Playing Piano Is Fun

Alice Chua

Book 1

Student: _____

Teacher: _____

© RHYTHM MP SDN. BHD. 2012

Published by
RHYTHM MP SDN. BHD.
1947, Lorong IKS Bukit Minyak 2,
Taman IKS Bukit Minyak, 14100 Simpang Ampat,
Penang, Malaysia.
Tel: +60 4 5050246 (Direct Line), +60 4 5073690 (Hunting Line)
Fax: +60 4 5050691
E-mail: rhythmmp@mphsb.com
Website: www.rhythmmp.com

ISBN 10: 967-985-616-X
ISBN 13: 978 967985616 3
Order No.: MPP-4003-01

Foreword

Playing Piano is Fun is a keyboard tutor series for beginners. It is designed to meet the developmental needs of children as they journey through the wonderful world of music. The tunes are specially composed by Alice Chua, and are based on the characters and subjects from the classic stories of *Alice's Adventures in Wonderland* and *Through the Looking-Glass* by Lewis Carroll. The literary experience is translated into the language of music with the intention of awakening the musical interests of children.

Playing Piano is Fun is a novel approach developed through the author's practical experience derived from teacher-pupil interaction. The large music font size captures the students' attention and helps them to focus. Meanwhile, pages are left intentionally without pictures to encourage students to further express their creativity by providing illustrations for the songs themselves. New elements are introduced incrementally and are incorporated progressively. Teacher's accompaniment is encouraged to enhance the musical experience, thus inspiring and motivating students. Some suggestions for the enhancement of the teaching elements can be found inside the front cover. In addition to playing piano, this series' unique approach includes listening, singing, transposing, harmonising, improvising and composing at an early stage.

A note from the author:

I wish pupils and teachers many fun and enjoyable music-making sessions with this series.

Yours musically,

Alice Chua, MA, FLCM, LLCM, Adv Dip Kodaly, Yamaha Teaching Cert. Grade 3.

About the Author

Alice is a passionate and enthusiastic musician, a versatile arranger, composer and music author. To this date, she has written many music books, used extensively in Asia and the United Kingdom. She is also an examiner with the London College of Music.

Whilst living in Malaysia and Singapore, Alice was Chief Music Instructor for Yamaha Music Asia. She opened new music schools in Singapore, Malaysia and Myanmar, and started music programs for pre-schoolers in Indonesia. This involved training teachers and designing music curricula suited specifically for each country. She frequently represented Malaysia in various international conferences hosted by Yamaha Music Foundation.

Now residing in London with her daughter, Alice divides her time between sharing her love of music with her students and invigilating examinations and competitions in Europe and the Far East. She believes that music should be played from memory, so that every child has the confidence to perform in any environment at any time, without needing to rely on a score. When children can express themselves freely in this way, it develops their ability to immediately engage their audience, and to derive from the music a personal sense of enjoyment.

Dedication

I would like to dedicate this series to my daughter Mitra and all my students, especially those who have chosen music as their profession.

I look back with fondness on our shared past, revel in our current projects and eagerly anticipate the future.

Contents

Date:_____

Introduction

♪ Finger Numbers

Let's learn the finger numbers.

Let's trace around your hands and mark on the finger numbers on page 8. You have drawn a hand chart!

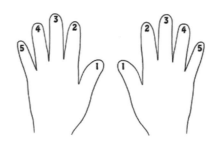

♪ The Piano

Black keys are grouped in twos and threes.

How many groups of two black keys can you find?

How many groups of three black keys can you find?

♪ Finding D Note

The D note is in the middle of the group of two black keys.

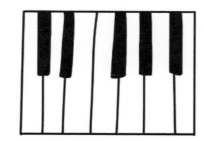

Let's find all the D notes on the piano.

Let's play D note with finger number two on your right hand, along with your teacher's accompaniment.

Let's find notes C, D, E, F and G on the piano.

Let's imitate your teacher's hand shape.

Now you are ready to copy your teacher's melodies.

♪ The Stave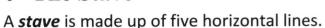

A *stave* is made up of five horizontal lines.

Let's number the lines on *Mummy Dinah Washing the Kittens* on page 11.

Hint: count from the bottom line.

♪ Treble Clef or G Clef

The *treble clef* is known as the *G clef*.

At this stage of study, the *treble clef* notes are being played by the right hand.

♪ Correct Sitting Posture

You need to check your sitting posture.

Your teacher will show you how to sit correctly.

Is the piano stool too near the piano for you to play comfortably?

Is the piano stool at the right height for you to play comfortably?

Is the piano stool at the centre of the keyboard?

♪ **Let's Trace**

Left hand

Right hand

♪ The Keyboard

Are you ready for a game on your paper keyboard?

Draw circles over the groups of two black keys.

Draw triangles over the groups of three black keys.

Find the D notes on the keyboard, and mark them in red.

Find the C notes on the keyboard, and mark them in blue.

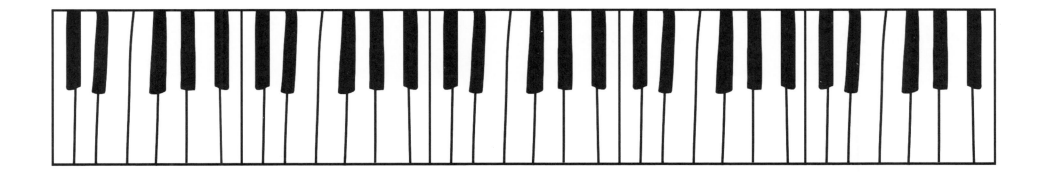

Date:_____

Part One

♪ Middle C

Middle C is written on a short line below the five horizontal lines of the **treble clef**. This short line is called the **ledger line**. Middle C is a **line note**.

♪ Time Name & Time Value 1

A **crotchet** ♩ has 1 count.

A **minim** ♩ has 2 counts, and lasts for 2 **crotchets**.

A **semibreve** o has 4 counts, and lasts for 4 **crotchets**.

♪ Games:

On page 11:

    a. Draw a circle around a **crotchet**.

    b. Draw a triangle over a **minim**.

    c. Draw a square over a **semibreve**.

♪ Pointers:

Are you playing with a good hand-shape?

Are you sitting comfortably?

Are you holding the **minims** to their full values?

Mummy Dinah Washing the Kittens

Alice Chua

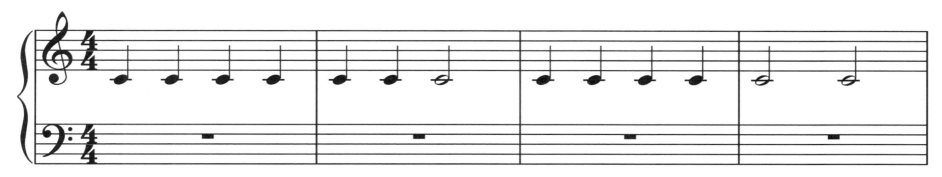

Alice's pet cat Dinah has two kittens - black Kitty & white Snowdrop.

♪ D Note

On the right of Middle C is the D note.

D is written touching the first line of the **treble clef stave**.

D is a **space note**.

♪ Bass Clef or F Clef

The **bass clef** is known as the **F clef**.

At this stage of study, the **bass clef** notes are played by the left hand.

♪ Games:

On page 13:

- a. How many D notes can you find?
- b. Circle the D **minims**.
- c. How many **bass clefs** can you find?

♪ Pointers:

Are you sitting comfortably?

Do you have a good hand shape?

Are you playing the notes smoothly? **Legato** is the Italian musical term for playing notes smoothly and connected.

Are you holding the semibreves to their full values?

Kitty Playing With Snowdrop

Alice Chua

Kitty and Snowdrop are best of friends.

Date:_____

♪ E Note

On the right of the D is the E note. E is written on the first line in the ***treble clef stave***. E is a ***line note***.

♪ Bar Rest

A ***bar rest*** is a bar of silence. A ***bar rest*** is written on the ***stave*** 'hanging' from the fourth line. A ***bar rest*** in the ***bass clef*** tells us that the left hand is 'resting'.

♪ Games:

On page 15:

    a. How many E notes can you find?

    b. Circle the E ***crotchets***.

    c. How many ***bar rests*** can you find?

    d. Circle the stepwise notes ***C-D-E***.

    e. Draw triangles over the D ***minims***.

♪ Pointers:

Do you have good sitting posture?

Are you playing with a good hand shape?

Are you playing ***legato***?

Are you holding the ***minims*** to their full values?

Curiouser and Curiouser

Alice Chua

Alice falls into the rabbit hole.
Try to play the E on the black key. Can you describe the mood?

♪ Notes C, D & E

The Garden of Live Flowers on page 17 is composed from
C-D-E. Their sol-fa names are **C – Do**, **D – Re** and **E – Mi**.

♪ Rhythm Name 1

A **crotchet** can be read as **ta**. A **minim** can be read as **ta-aa**.

♪ Play & Sing Along

Let's play and sing in letter names.
Let's play and sing in sol-fa names.
Let's play and sing in rhythm names.

♪ Games:

On page 17:

    a. Circle the stepwise notes **E-D-C**.
    b. Draw a triangle over each **minim**.
    c. Draw a square over the Middle C **crotchets**.

♪ Pointers:

Do you have good sitting posture?
Do you have a good hand-shape?
Are you holding the **minims** to their full value?

The Garden of Live Flowers

Alice Chua

Alice enters the garden of Live Flowers.
Who does Alice meet in the Garden of Live Flowers?

♪ Notes C, D & E

The Large Flower Bed is also composed of the stepwise notes **C-D-E**.

♪ Play & Sing Along

Let's play and sing in letter names.

Let's play and sing in sol-fa names.

Let's play and sing in rhythm names.

♪ Games:

1) Circle the stepwise notes **E-D-C** on page 19.
2) Underline the correct answer:
   a. A *minim* equals 2 / 3 / 4 *crotchets*.
   b. A *semibreve* equals 2 / 3 / 4 *crotchets*.
   c. A *semibreve* equals 2 / 3 / 4 *minims*.

♪ Pointers:

Are you sitting in the correct posture?

Is the piano stool at the right distance from the piano?

Is the piano stool at the right height for you?

Do you have a good hand shape?

Are you playing *legato*?

The Large Flower Bed

Alice Chua

Name some flowers in the large flower bed.

Date:_____

♪ Notes C, D & E

The Willow-Tree is also composed of these notes.

♪ Rhythm Name 2

A *semibreve* can be read as *ta-aa-aa-aa*.

♪ Play & Sing Along

Let's play and sing in letter names.
Let's play and sing in sol-fa names.
Let's play and sing in rhythm names.

Let's play eight notes higher. Can you hear the difference in pitch? You have played an *octave* higher! The Willow-Tree is swaying in the breeze!

♪ Games:

1) Circle the stepwise notes *C-D-E* on page 21.
2) Give the rhythm name for a *crotchet*.
3) Give the rhythm name for a *minim*.

♪ Pointer:

Are you playing the repeated notes to their full values?

The Willow-Tree

Alice Chua

Can you draw a tall Willow-Tree?

♪ Notes C, D & E

Many tunes can be composed from just three stepwise notes.

♪ Play & Sing Along

Let's play and sing in letter names.

Let's play and sing in sol-fa names.

Let's play and sing in rhythm names.

Let's play page 23 an **octave** higher. Can you hear the difference in pitch?

♪ Games:

1) Circle the stepwise notes **E-D-C** on page 23.
2) How many notes are in an **octave**?
3) How do you verbalise
   a. **Crotchets**?
   b. **Minims**?
   c. **Semibreves**?

♪ Pointers:

Do you have good sitting posture?

Are you holding the **semibreves** to their full values?

Tiger-Lily Says 'We Can Talk'

Alice Chua

Tiger-Lily is talking to Alice.

Date:_____

♪ F Note

On the right of E is the F note. F is written between the first and second lines in the **treble clef stave**. F is a **space note**. F can be sung as **Fa**.

♪ Bars and Bar-Lines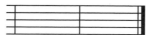

Bar-lines are vertical lines drawn on the stave. A **bar** is the space between two **bar-lines**. At the end of the music, there is a pair of vertical lines called the **Double Bar-Line**.

♪ Play & Sing Along:

Let's play *The Willow-Tree Barks* one **octave** higher. Now let's play two **octaves** higher.

♪ Games:

On page 25:

    a. Circle the F **crotchets**.

    b. How many **bars** can you find?

♪ Pointers:

Are you paying close attention to a good hand shape?
Are you playing **legato**?

The Willow-Tree Barks

Alice Chua

Rose explains that the Willow-Tree is barking because it has bark.

Date:_____

♪ Notes C, D, E & F

The composition on page 27 is based on the repetition of the rhythmic pattern '*te-te*, *te-te*, *ta*, *ta*'.

♪ Time Name & Time Value 2

A *quaver* ♪ equals half a *crotchet*.

♪ Rhythm Name 3

A *quaver* can be read as *te*, two *quavers* as *te-te*.

♪ Play & Sing Along

Let's play and sing in letter names.

Let's clap and sing the rhythm.

♪ Games:

On page 27:

  a. How many F notes can you find?

  b. Circle the stepwise notes *D-E-F*.

  c. Draw triangles over the F *crotchets*.

♪ Pointers:

Are you clapping the *quavers* evenly?

Are you holding the *semibreves* to their full values?

The Willow-Tree Says 'Bough-Wough'

Alice Chua

Daisy explains that the Willow-Tree says 'Bough-Wough' because it has boughs.

Date:_____

♪ Notes C, D, E & F

This composition is based on the stepwise notes **D-E-F**.

♪ Play & Sing Along

Let's play and sing in letter names.

Let's play and sing in sol-fa names.

Let's clap and sing in rhythm names.

♪ Games:

1) On page 29:
   a. How many F notes can you find?
   b. Circle the stepwise notes **D-E-F**.
2) Circle the **double bar-line**.
3) Draw triangles over the groups of four **quavers**.
4) Underline the correct answer:
   a. A **semibreve** equals 2 / 3 / 4 **crotchets**.
   b. A **semibreve** equals 2 / 3 / 4 **minims**.
   c. A **minim** equals 2 / 3 / 4 **crotchets**.

♪ Pointers:

Are you clapping and singing the **quavers** evenly?

Are you playing the **quaver** and **crotchet** values accurately?

The Daisies' Shrill Voices

Alice Chua

The Daisies all talk at the same time.

♪ G Note

On the right of the F is the G note. G is written on the second line in the **treble clef stave**. G is a **line note**. G can be sung as **So**.

♪ Play & Sing Along

Let's play and sing in letter names.

Let's play and sing in sol-fa names.

Let's play *The Pink Daisies* an **octave** lower with your left hand. Can you hear the difference in pitch? Can you imagine a cello playing these eight bars?

♪ Games:

1) On page 31:
    a. How many G notes can you find?
    b. Circle the stepwise notes **G-F-E**.
2) Underline the correct answer:
    a. A **crotchet** equals 2 / 3 / 4 **quavers**.
    b. A **minim** equals 2 / 3 / 4 **quavers**.

♪ Pointer:

Remember: poor posture prevents poetic performance.

The Pink Daisies

Alice Chua

Can you draw some pink daisies?

Date:_____

♪ Notes C, D, E, F & G

This composition is based on the stepwise notes *E-F-G.*

♪ Time Signature

Time signature is written after the clef. The top number tells us the **number** of beats in a **bar**. The bottom number tells us the **kind** of beats in a **bar**.

♪ Play & Sing Along

Let's play this tune now, starting on G. Can you hear the difference in pitch? You are now playing in G hand position! Can you express your mood to your teacher?

♪ Games:

On page 33:

    a. Circle the stepwise notes *E-F-G.*

    b. What is the *time signature*?

♪ Pointers:

Are you placing your thumb on Middle C? (This is the Middle C hand position).

Are you holding the **semibreves** to their full values?

Sleepy Violet

Alice Chua

Violet is usually asleep in the Garden of Live Flowers.

Date:_____

♪ Notes C, D, E, F & G

The composition on page 35 is based on two stepwise patterns: *D-E-F* and *E-F-G*.

♪ Play & Sing Along

Let's play and sing in letter names.

Let's play and sing in sol-fa names.

Let's play and sing in rhythm names.

♪ Games:

1) On page 35:
    a. How many E *crotchets* can you find?
    b. How many E *quavers* can you find?
    c. Circle the stepwise notes *D-E-F*.
    d. Draw a triangle over the stepwise notes *E-F-G*.
2) Underline the correct answer:
    Four *quavers* equal 2 / 3 / 4 *crotchets*.

♪ Pointers:

Are you clapping the *quavers* evenly?

Are you playing the *crotchets* accurately?

Are you holding the last *minim* to its full value?

She's Redder

Alice Chua

Who is redder than Alice?

♪ Notes C, D, E, F & G

Nine Spikes Crown is on page 38.

♪ Play & Sing Along

Let's play and sing in letter names.

Let's play and sing in sol-fa names.

Let's play from memory.

♪ Games:

1) Draw a crown on page 37.

2) Underline the correct answer:
   a. A *semibreve* equals 2 / 3 / 4 *minims*.
   b. A *semibreve* equals 2 / 3 / 4 *crotchets*.
   c. A *minim* equals 2 / 3 / 4 *crotchets*.
   d. A *crotchet* equals 2 / 3 / 4 *quavers*.
   e. A *minim* equals 2 / 3 / 4 *quavers*.

♪ Pointers:

Do you have good sitting posture?

Are you playing with a good hand shape?

Are you playing the *semibreves* to their full values?

Are you playing the *quavers* evenly?

♪ **Can you draw the Red Queen's crown?**

Nine Spikes Crown

Alice Chua

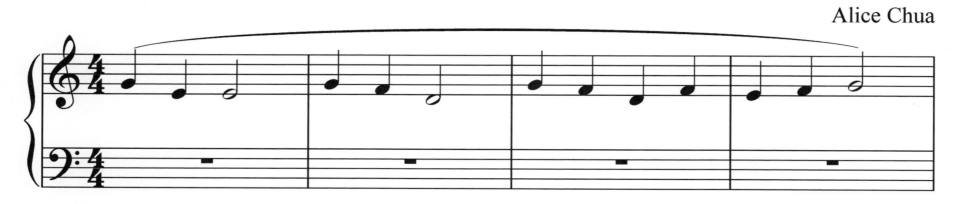

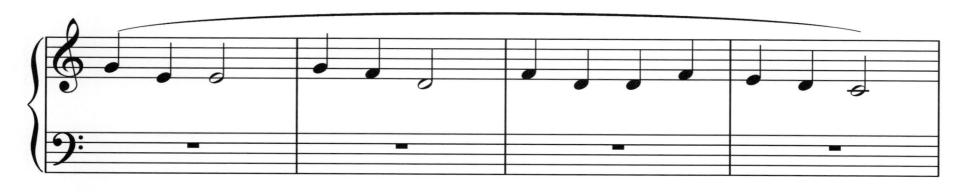

Who is wearing the nine spikes crown?

Draw the Red Queen wearing the nine spikes crown.

Date:_____

♪ Notes C, D, E, F & G

Happy Talking Flowers can be more enjoyable with lyrics added to it. Can you compose lyrics for this tune? Look inside the cover for suggestions.

♪ Crotchet Rest

A **crotchet rest** ‚ has 1 count.

♪ Play & Sing Along

Let's play and sing in letter names.

Let's play and sing in sol-fa names.

Enjoy singing your lyrics to this merry tune.

♪ Games:

On page 41:

    a. Circle the stepwise notes **G-F-G**.

    b. Draw a triangle over the **crotchet rest**.

♪ Pointers:

Are you playing and clapping the **quavers** evenly?

Did you remember to **rest** at the last beat of bar 8?

Are you playing **legato**?

Happy Talking Flowers

Alice Chua

What are the Talking Flowers talking about?

Part Two

♪ Notes G, A, B & Middle C in the Bass Clef

Middle C is on a **ledger line** above the top line of the **bass clef stave**. Place the thumb of your left hand on Middle C. Now place finger 2 on B, finger 3 on A, finger 4 on G, and finger 5 on F. This is Middle C hand position. You are ready to play *Larkspur's Announcement.*

♪ Play & Sing Along

Let's play and sing with words.

Let's play and sing in letter names.

♪ Games:

On page 43:

    a. Circle the stepwise notes **G-A-B-C**.

    b. Draw triangles over the D **minims**.

♪ Pointers:

Are both hands in Middle C position before you start?

Are you playing each note clearly?

Larkspur's Announcement

Alice Chua

What is Larkspur's announcement?

44

Date:_____

♪ Notes G, A, B & Middle C in the Bass Clef

Prepare the same hand position as *Larkspur's Announcement*.

♪ Play & Sing Along

Let's play and sing in letter names.

Let's play and sing in rhythm names.

♪ Games:

1) Underline the correct answer:

   A **crotchet** equals 2 / 3 / 4 **quavers**.

2) On page 45:

   a. Circle the stepwise notes **G-F-E-D**.

   b. Circle the stepwise notes **C-B-A-G**.

   c. Draw triangles over the E notes in the **treble clef**.

♪ Pointers:

Are both hands in position before you start playing?

Are you sitting comfortably?

Do you have a good hand shape?

Are you playing **legato**?

Are you holding the **minims** to their full values?

Thump, Thump, Thump!

Alice Chua

Who is making the thumping sound?

♪ Notes G, A, B & Middle C in the Bass Clef

Prepare the same hand position as *Thump, Thump, Thump!*

♪ Time Name & Time Value 3

A ***dotted minim*** has three counts.

♪ Rhythm Name 4

A ***dotted minim*** can be read as ***ta-aa-aa***.

♪ Play & Sing Along

Let's play and sing in letter names.

Let's play and sing in rhythm names.

♪ Games:

On page 47:

    a. Draw triangles over Middle C notes in the ***bass clef***.

    b. Name the other notes in the ***bass clef***.

    c. Circle the stepwise notes ***C-B-A-G***.

    d. Circle the stepwise notes ***G-A-B-C***.

♪ Pointers:

Are you observing the rest in ***bar*** 8?

Are you playing the ***semibreve*** to its full value?

The Arrival of the Red Queen

Alice Chua

Larkspur announces the arrival of the Red Queen.

♪ Phrase Marking

You have seen lines drawn above some notes in tunes that you have played. These lines are called **phrase markings**. Notes within a phrase must be played smoothly (**legato**).

♪ Play & Sing Along

Let's play and sing in letter names.

Let's sing and take a breath at the end of each phrase. Your teacher will show you.

♪ Games:

1) On page 49:
    a. How many **phrases** can you find?
    b. Circle the stepwise notes **G-F-G**.
2) Underline the correct answers:
    a. A **dotted minim** equals 2 / 3 / 4 **crotchets**.
    b. A **crotchet** equals 2 / 3 / 4 **quavers**.
    c. A **dotted minim** equals 2 / 4 / 6 **quavers**.

♪ Pointers:

Are your hands in the correct position before you start?

Are you playing the notes within the **phrases** smoothly?

The Tall Red Queen

Alice Chua

The grand entrance of the Red Queen.

The Game of Looking-Glass Chess

Alice Chua

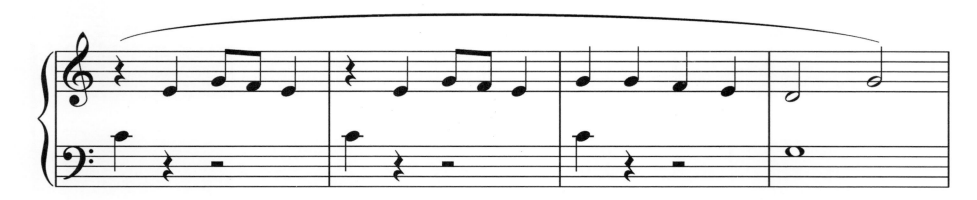

Alice wishes to play a game of Looking-Glass chess.

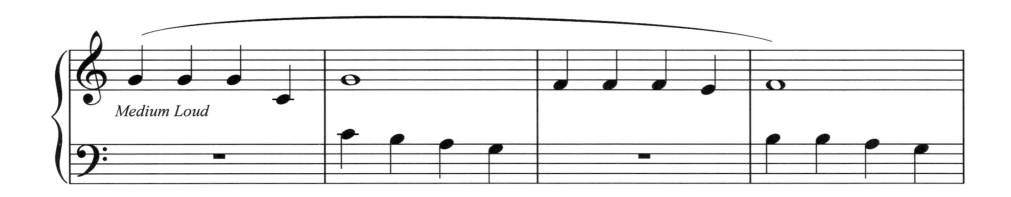

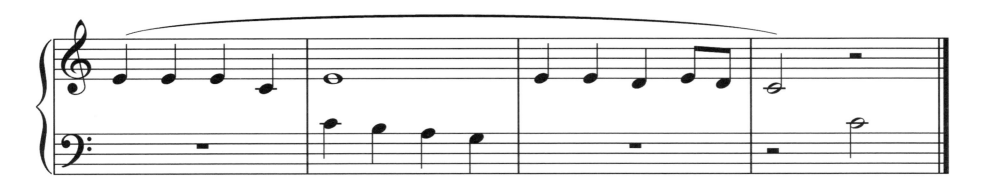

The Red Queen appoints Alice to be a white pawn.

The White Pawn

Moderately

Alice Chua

Dots above or below notes are called *staccato* markings. Play the notes short.

The White Pawn goes two squares ahead in its first move.

The Fourth Square

Alice Chua

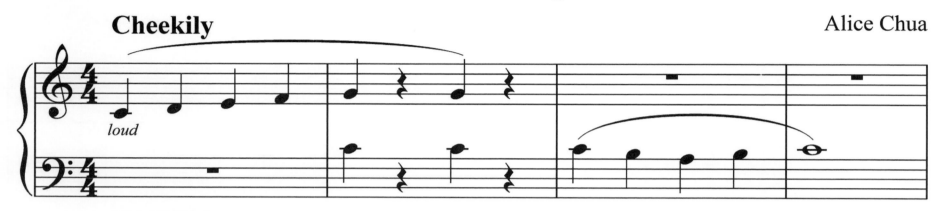

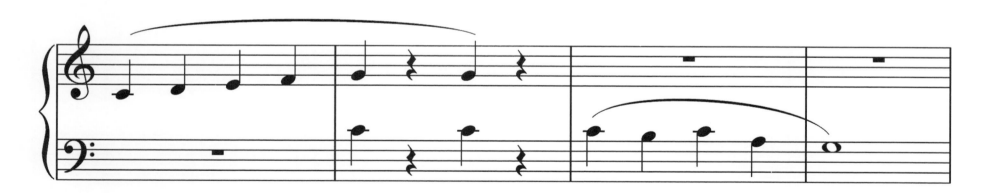

The fourth square belongs to Tweedledum ......

Tweedledee

.... and Tweedledee.

The White Knight

Steadily

Alice Chua

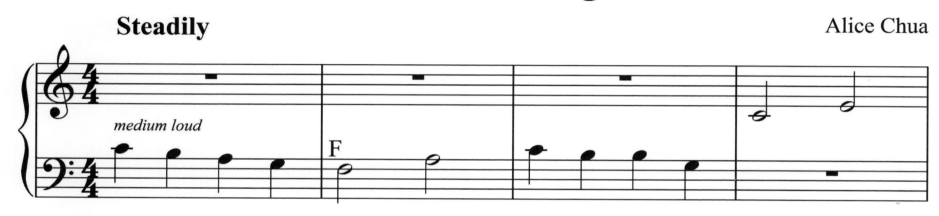

Alice will meet the White Knight at the seventh square.

The White Knight will guide Alice to the eighth square.
The new note is F in the bass clef. Can you circle all the F notes?

All Shall be Queens

Piano Duet (Secondo)

Alice Chua

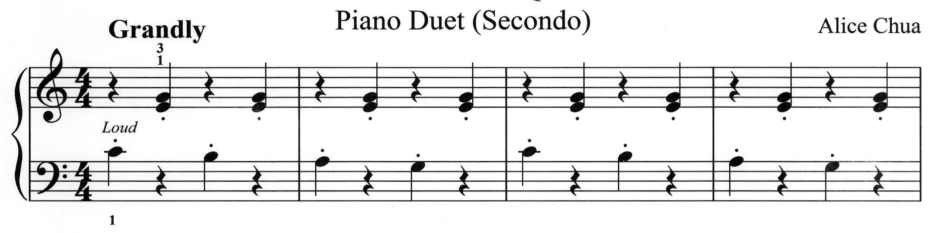

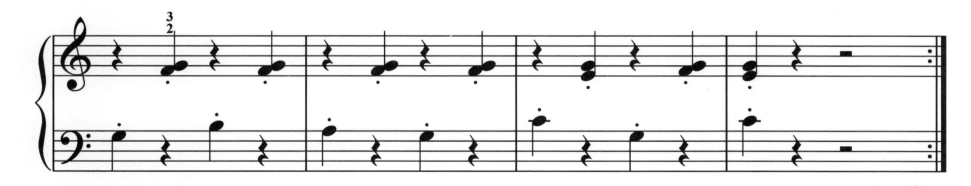

Who are the three Queens?

All Shall be Queens

Piano Duet (Primo)

Alice Chua

Grandly

To play both hands one octave higher

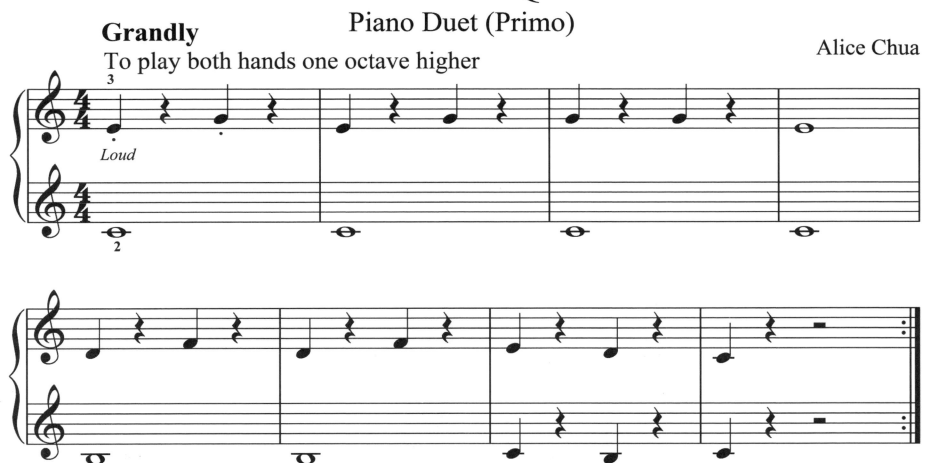

Loud

Let's mark all the crotchets with *staccato* markings.

This passage is to be repeated. Your teacher will show you the repeat sign.

Game 1

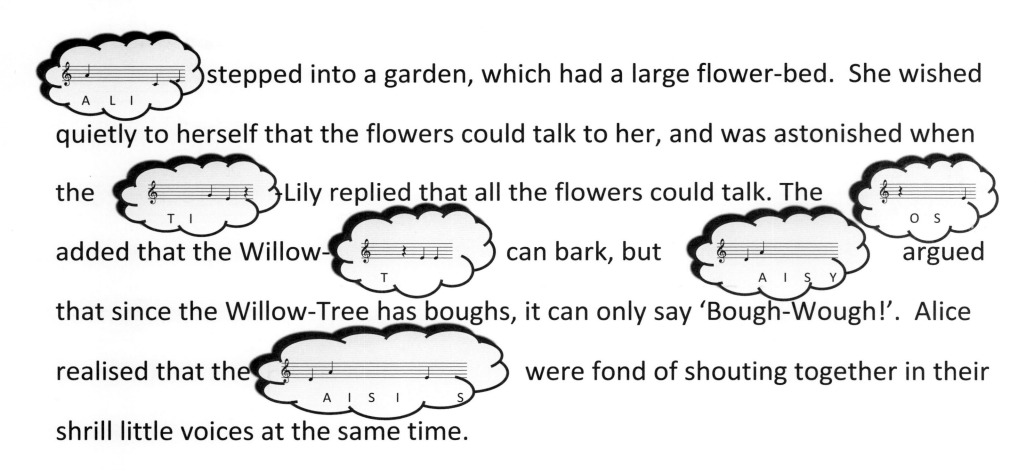stepped into a garden, which had a large flower-bed. She wished quietly to herself that the flowers could talk to her, and was astonished when the Lily replied that all the flowers could talk. The added that the Willow- can bark, but argued that since the Willow-Tree has boughs, it can only say 'Bough-Wough!'. Alice realised that the were fond of shouting together in their shrill little voices at the same time.

Game 2

The (__ __) T I -Lily was not happy with the Sleepy (__ __) V I O L T for encouraging the (__ __) O S to tease Alice. The (__ __) O S mistook Alice for a flower, and talked about another flower like Alice, who was redder and wore nine spikes on her head. The (__ __) L A K S P U loudly announced the arrival of the (__ __) Queen, and Alice remarked that she had grown a head taller since they last met. The (__ __) O S explained that the fresh air in the Garden of Live Flowers caused magical growth.